The SESAME STREET SONG BOOK

WORDS AND MUSIC BY
JOE RAPOSO AND **JEFFREY MOSS**

ARRANGEMENTS BY SY OLIVER

·

ILLUSTRATED BY LORETTA TREZZO

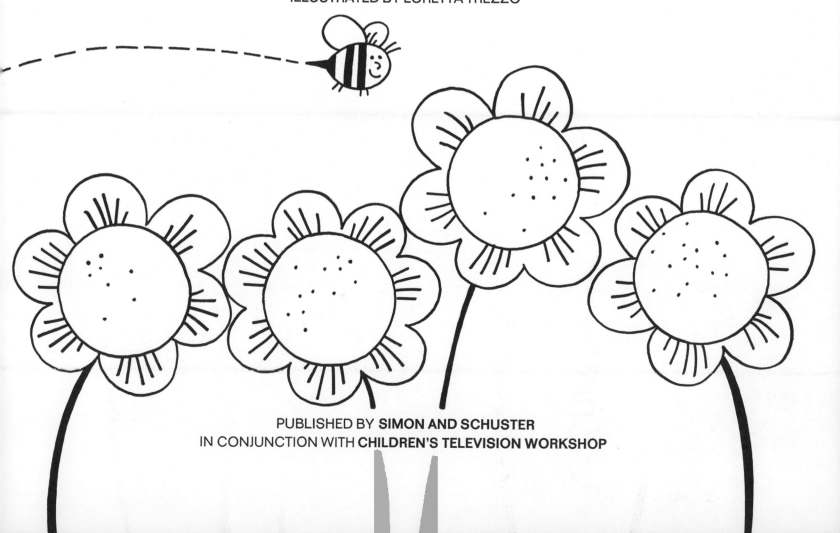

PUBLISHED BY **SIMON AND SCHUSTER**
IN CONJUNCTION WITH **CHILDREN'S TELEVISION WORKSHOP**

Published by Simon and Schuster

Rockefeller Center, 630 Fifth Avenue

New York, New York 10020

FIRST PRINTING

SBN 671-21036-X

Library of Congress Catalog Card Number: 74-161217

Manufactured in the United States of America

Printed by The Murray Printing Company, Forge Village, Mass.

CONTENTS

SESAME STREET

Words by Bruce Hart · Music by Joe Raposo

1. Sun-ny day sweep-in' the clouds a-way on my way to where the air is sweet. Can you
2. Come and play! Ev'-ry-thing's A-O-kay. Friend-ly neigh-bors there, that's where we meet. Can you

7

clouds_ a - way   on_ my   way   to where the

air is_ sweet._   Can you tell   me how   to get,   how to get   to

Se - sa - me   Street?_____   how   to get   to   Se - sa - me   Street?_____

___ how   to get   to   Se - sa - me Street?_____

AB-C-DEF-GHI

Words by Joe Raposo and Jon Stone · Music by Joe Raposo

AB - C -DEF- GHI - J - KL- M -NOP- QR-STUV- WX- YZ_____ is the

most re-mar-ka-ble word I've ev – er seen._____

10

AB - C - DEF - GHI - J - KL - M - NOP - QR - STUV - WX - YZ? _____ I
wish I knew ex - act - ly what I mean. _____ It
starts out ___ like an "A" word, ___ as an - y - one can see, ___ but
some - where there in the mid - dle, it gets aw - f'ly "QR" to me.

11

AB - C - DEF - GHI - J - KL - M - NOP - QR - STUV - WX - YZ! _____ If I

ev - er find out just what this word can mean, _____ I'll be the

smar - test bird the world has ev - er seen. _____

Interlude a tempo *Slower* SPOKEN

It might be kind of an e-le-phant, _ or a

12

fun - ny kind of ka - zoo, or a strange, ex - ot - ic tur - tle_____ that you

nev - er see in a zoo. It might be a kind of a

dog - gie, or a par - tic - u - lar shade of blue, or

may - be a pret - ty flow-er?___ Naah, not with a name like that uh, uh!

CIRCLES

Rock, with a steady beat

Words and music by Jeffrey Moss

1. See the sun up— in the sky?_ Well, it's a cir - cle.
2. See a wheel on a rol - ler skate?_ Well, it's a cir - cle.

See a hu - la hoop roll by?_ Well, it's a cir - cle.
See a cook - ie on a plate?_ Well, it's a cir - cle.

14

See the sun up in the sky;__ see a hu-la
See a wheel on a rol-ler skate;__ see a cook-ie

hoop roll by,__ round as a fresh-baked ap-ple pie, And it's a cir-cle.
on a plate. Boy, that__ cook-ie sure is great, And it's a cir-cle.

(sim.)

See that great big man-hole cov-er ly-ing on the ground? It's

15

not a square or tri-an-gle;__ It's big and flat and round,__ And it's a

cir-cle.

See a great big let-ter "O"?__ Well, it's a cir-cle.

See a boun-cy ball? You know__ that it's a

cir - cle.   I like that great big let - ter "O";—   I

like that boun - cy ball, and so___ the shape that I like

best, you know,—Well, it's a cir - cle.   Yeah, it's a

cir - cle._____ Oh, yeah!

FIVE PEOPLE IN MY FAMILY

Words and music by Jeffrey Moss

Soft Shoe

Oh, I've got

A tempo

1. five peo-ple in my fam'-ly, and there's not one of them I'd
2. five fin-gers on my left hand; I've got five fin-gers on my

swap. There is a sis-ter, and two broth-ers, and a
right. Five fin-gers help me wave good mor-ning, Help me

18

J JUMP

Words and music by Joe Raposo

"J" jump joy - ful, jum - ble a - round, ___ jun - i - per Jan ___ Jane

John. "J" jump joy - ful jum - ble a - round, ___

jack - in -the - box__ jump - in' all o -ver town.__ Jin - gle, jan - gle, junk,

sum - mer day,__ big "J" swing-in', fly - in', sing-in'! "J" jump joy - ful,

jum - ble a - round,__ on a just nice day, with the jump - in'-est jays in

town. town.

21

I'VE GOT TWO

Words by Jeffrey Moss · Music by Joe Raposo

I've got two eyes. One, two. They're both the same size. One, two. I've got two eyes, _____ and they're both the same size.

22

I've got two ears. One, two._ They help me hear.

One, two._ I've got two ears; they help me hear. I've got two eyes,____

and they're both the same size. Two

arms have I. One, two._ I can hold them up high. One, two._ Two

Two hands have I.
   One, two.
They can wave goodbye.
   One, two.
Two hands have I;
   they can wave goodbye.
Two arms have I;
   I can hold them high.
I've got two ears to help me hear.
I've got two eyes,
   and they're both the same size.

I've got two knees.
   One, two.
They're as round as you please.
   One, two.
I've got two knees;
   they're as round as you please.
Two hands have I;
   they can wave goodbye.
Two arms have I;
   I can hold them up high.
I've got two ears to help me hear.
I've got two eyes,
   and they're both the same size.

I've got two feet.
   One, two.
They can walk down the street.
   One, two.
I've got two feet;
   they can walk down the street.
I've got two knees;
   they're as round as you please.
Two hands have I;
   they can wave goodbye.
Two arms have I;
   I can hold them up high.
I've got two ears to help me hear.
I've got two eyes,
   and they're both the same size.

KIDS

Words and music by Joe Raposo

Cats have kit-tens,___ dog-gies have pups,

25

hor - ses have pret - ty foals and sheep have lambs.

Cows have calves, and I bet you did-n't know that el - e-phants have calves too.— Li - ons and leop-ards have cubs, which is the prop - er thing for them to do. Pea-cocks have chicks, — deer have fawns,

ducks have duck-lings, of-ten pad-ding round on lawns.

Pigs have pig-lets, and in case you did-n't know, I've a-noth-er fact for

you:_____ Goats have kids, like peo-ple have kids, Like me._____

____ and you_____

RIGHT IN THE MIDDLE OF MY FACE

Words and music by Jeffrey Moss

1. Right in the mid-dle of my face, right in its ver-y spec-ial
2. nose, I am sure you will a-gree, there are two things that help me
3. Right up a-bove my chin there is a thing I put food

place, is a thing that helps me sneeze and breathe as
see. I use them when I look at you, and you use
in. It helps me when talk, it helps me chew, and then it

And so do you.___ 2. A-bove my

And so do you.___

And so do

you.___

SONG OF FIVE

Words and music by Joe Raposo

Rock

One, two, three, four, five, six, se-ven, eight, nine, ten.

31

UP AND DOWN

Words and music by Jeffrey Moss

Oh, I look 1. up and see a bir - die fly - ing
2. up and see an air-plane fly - ing,
3. up and see the ceil – ing, and there's

high and free.__ Well, I look down, and then the side__ walk is
yes I do.__ Well, I look down and see my foot, and then I
one thing more:__ Well, I look down and see the rug, and then I

34

35

WHAT MAKES MUSIC ?

Words and music by Joe Raposo

36

When you're hap-py on the in-side, ev-'ry-thing you hear is mu-sic. An old tin can, that's mu-sic._____ A fry-ing pan, that's mu-sic._____ An e-lec-tric fan that's mu-sic._____ A pa-per and a comb, a

wash - board and a bone, a buck - et that you bang on or a

ring - ing tel - e - phone. What makes mu - sic?

An - y - thing makes mu - sic! When your heart is o - pen wide, then

ev' - ry - thing a - round is mu - sic. And mu - sic fills the

ONE OF THESE THINGS

Words and music by Joe Raposo

One of these things is not like the oth - ers;

one of these things just does - n't be - long. Can you tell which thing is

not like the oth - ers by the time I fin - ish my song?

Hum, and show different objects. _____

Did you

guess which thing is not like the oth-ers? Did you guess real hard, with

all of your might? If you guessed this thing is not like the oth-ers, then you're

ab-so-lute-ly___ right! right!

42

THE PEOPLE IN YOUR NEIGHBORHOOD

Words and music by Jeffrey Moss

Oh,___ 1. who___ are the peo – ple in your
2. post-man is a per – son in your

neigh-bor-hood, in your neigh-bor-hood, in your neigh – bor – hood? Oh,
neigh-bor-hood, in your neigh-bor-hood, in your neigh – bor – hood. The

who___ are the peo – ple in your neigh-bor-hood, the peo – ple that you meet each
post-man is a per – son in your neigh-bor-hood, a per – son that you meet each

fire-man is a per-son in your neigh-bor-hood, in your neigh-bor-hood, in your

neigh - bor - hood, and a post-man is a per - son in your neigh-bor-hood. They're the

peo - ple that you meet when you're walk-ing down the street; they're the peo - ple that you

meet each day.

EVERYBODY WASH

Words and music by Joe Raposo

Lyrics:

Ev -'ry bo - dy wash your hands.

Ev -'ry bo - dy wash your face.

46

O. K. Ev'-ry-bo-dy   wash your an - kles.

O. K.

Wash your ev'-ry-thing.

GOIN' FOR A RIDE

Words and music by Jeffrey Moss

Oh, I'm go - in' for a 1. ride, gon - na sit be-hind the
2. ride, and I'm nev - er com - ing
3. ride, gon - na sail the o - cean

wheel, Gon - na drive a - long the road.
back. Gon - na be an en - gi - neer,
blue, and I'm gon - na be a cap - tain

Oh, how hap-py I will feel!
gon-na speed a-long the track.
and I'm gon-na have a crew.

And I'm gon-na toot my
And you'll hear my whis-tle
Gon-na sail the sev-en

horn,
blow,
seas;

gon-na trav-el near and far,
and I'm hap-py to ex-plain
on the wa-ter I will float,

'cause I'm go-in' for a ride,
that I'm go-in' for a ride,
'cause I'm go-in' for a ride,

go-in' ri-din' in a
go-in' ri-din' in a
and I'm ri-din' in a

49

boat.   Yes, I'm go - in' for   a   ride (Beep - Beep!)

Yes, I'm go - in' for   a   ride (Woo - Woo!),   yes, I'm go - in' for   a

ride (Toot - Toot!)   Yes, I'm go - in' for   a   ride! _____

MY NAME

Rock, with energy

Words and music by Jeffrey Moss

with Pedal

1. My name's (Da-vid). That's a fine_ name. It's not your_ name, but it's
2. Your name's (Su-san). That's a fine_ name. It's not my_ name, but it's

fine just the same. I stand up tall, and I say it loud-ly:
fine just the same. Stand up tall, and_ say it loud-ly:

(Da-vid) is my name._ Oh yeah, it's my name,_ and I
(Su-san) is my name._

don't wan-na change it. It's my name,— and I like it real fine,— yeah!

My name,— there ain't no one can take it. (Da-vid's) my name, and I'm
(Su-san's)

1

proud that it's mine.

2

mine.

RUB YOUR TUMMY

Words by Dave Connell · Music by Joe Raposo

1. Rub your tum-my, just like this. Rub it all day long.___
2. Pat your head,___ just like this. Pat it all day long.___

Rub your tum-my, rub it hard, while we sing our song.___
Pat your head,___ but not too hard, and sing our sil-ly song.___

54

Rub, rub, rub,— rub, rub, rub, rub,— rub, rub, rub, rub,— rub,
Pat, pat, pat,— pat, pat, pat, pat,— pat, pat, pat, pat,— pat,

rub, rub, rub,— rub, rub, rub, rub,— rub, rub. Play and sing a - long.
pat, pat, pat,— pat, pat, pat, pat,— pat, pat. Sing our sil - ly song.

Rub your tum-my,—

pat your head.— Play and sing a - long——

as we sing our ve - ry ve - ry mer - ry, sil - ly song. ___

Clap your hands, just like this. ___ Clap 'em all day long.

___ Clap your hands, ___ one, two, three, ___

while we sing our song. ___ (CLAP) ___

WHAT CAN I DO?

Words and music by Joe Raposo

What can I do?

1. What can I be?
2. What can you do?

58

59

SURPRISE!

Rock n' roll - Moderato

Words and music by Jeffrey Moss

Ooh wah doo, ooh wah doo — bee yoo, ooh wah doo, sur-prise! —

Ooh wah doo, ooh wah doo — bee yoo, ooh wah doo, sur-prise! —

60

some - thing sud-den-ly hap - pens and you can't be - lieve your ey - es,_____

1ST TENOR, 2ND TENOR, BASS

Ooh wah doo - ooh wah doo bee you, ooh wah doo, sur-prise!

_____ it's a sur - pri - i - ise!

LEAD—1ST TEN., 2ND, BASS

1, 2

Fine

LEAD SINGER

A sur -

A sur - sur - pri - ise!_____

dim. - - - -

subito

ff

mp

62

A FACE

Words and music by Joe Raposo

Light Bossa Nova

A face can be up, a face can be down, A face can be as fun-ny as the face of a clown.___ A

face can show just__ how you feel in-side,__ When your eyes o-pen

up__ and your smile__ o-pens wide.____ Your eyes could be brown, your

eyes could be blue, But there's nev-er ev-er an-y oth-er

face just like you.__ And when you're sad__ or cry-ing__ and you

64

HIGH
MIDDLE
LOW

Words by Emily Kaplin · Music by Jeffrey Moss

Moderato

with Pedal

HIGH VOICE

I   can on - ly sing the high part;   it's   the on - ly part I

know.   And when I   sing the   high part,   this is how I

la   la,   la   la, la la la la la.

LOW VOICE

I   can on-ly sing the low part, low part; it's   the on-ly part I

know, I know. And when I sing the low, low part,   this is how I   go:

La   la, la la la la, la la, la la, la   la, la la la la la.

But when we put them all to-geth-er, to-geth-er I am sure you will a-

gree, a-gree, the whole sounds bet-ter than the parts, as you can plain-ly see:

La la, la la la la, la la,_____ la la, la la la la, la, la la la la!

69

WHAT DO I DO WHEN I'M ALONE?

Words and music by Jeffrey Moss

Slowly and gently

What do I do when I'm a-lone? Well,

(with Pedal)

some-times I sing a lit-tle song. La - la- la-la - la - la!

sim.

That is the song I sing. What do I do when I'm a-
lone? Well, some - times I do a lit - tle dance. I
jump and I hop, hop, hop; that is my lit - tle dance. And
some - times when I'm all a - lone, I pre - tend that I can fly,

71

and I touch all the clouds, and I wave to the bir-dies as

they pass by._____ But some-times when I am all a - lone, well,

some - times I feel a lit-tle sad 'cause there's no - one to share my

song, no - one to fly with me. So

some-times when I am all a - lone, I think of how hap-py I would
be if I was - n't a - lone and you were here with
me.

SOMEONE NICE

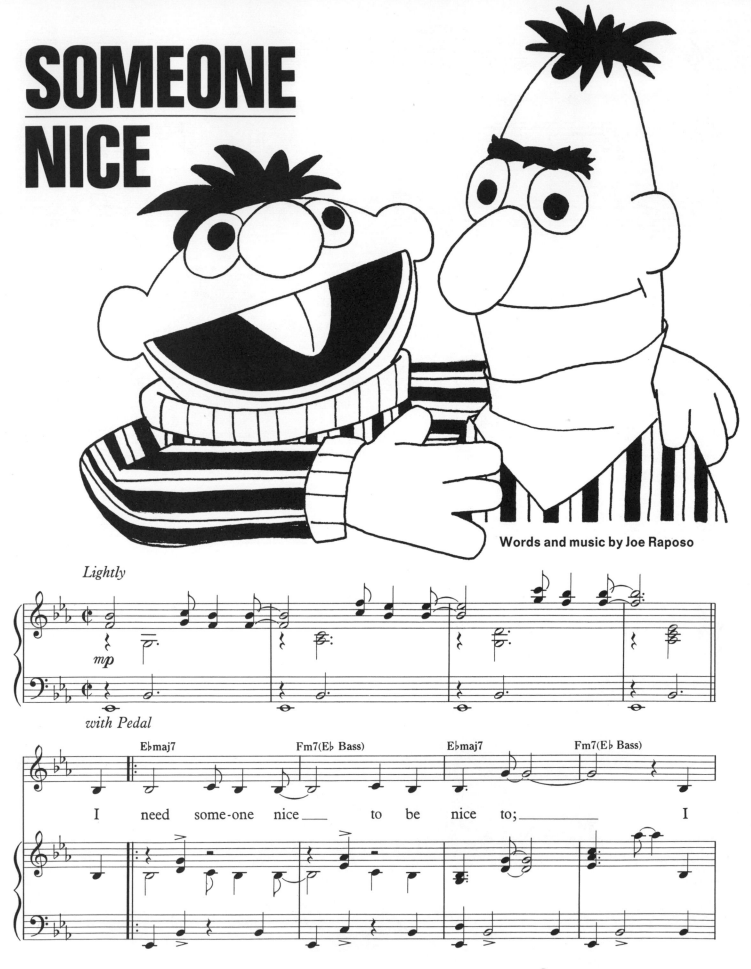

Words and music by Joe Raposo

Lightly

with Pedal

Ebmaj7   Fm7(Eb Bass)   Ebmaj7   Fm7(Eb Bass)

I need some-one nice ___ to be nice to; _____ I

76

some - one luck - y,____ who'll know he's luck - y when he knows I'll

need some-one nice____ to be nice to,_____ and

I'll be nee - ding some - one nice like that my whole life

through.   I through._____

EVERYONE MAKES MISTAKES

Words and music by Jeffrey Moss

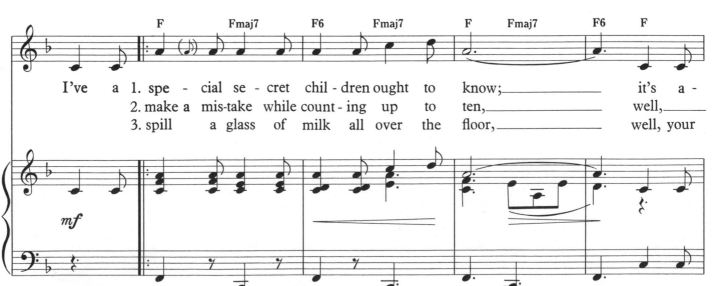

I've a 1. spe - cial se - cret chil - dren ought to know;_____ it's a-
2. make a mis-take while count - ing up to ten,_____ well,_____
3. spill a glass of milk all over the floor,_____ well, your

78

bout the lit - tle mis - takes you make as you be - gin to grow. If you
don't get mad__ and don't be sad; just start to count a - gain. And__
mom and dad__ still like you just as much as they did be - fore, 'cause when

make a mis - take, you should - n't start to cry.__ Mis -
if you should on - ly get to eight or nine,__ I'm
Moth - er and Dad were just as small as you,__ I'll

takes are not so bad, and here is why:__ Oh,
still your friend and I still like you fine. __ 'Cause
bet that they knocked their milk o - ver too. __ 'Cause

79

If you you._____ If ev-'ry-one in the whole wide world makes mis-takes, Then why_____ can't_____ you?_____

BEIN' GREEN

Words and music by Joe Raposo

It's not that ea - sy be - in' green,

hav - ing to spend each day the col - or of the leaves,

82

when I think it could be ni-cer be-in' red, or yel-low, or

gold, or some-thing much more col-or-ful like that. It's not

ea-sy be-in' green. It seems you blend in with so man-y oth-er

or-di-na-ry things, and peo-ple tend to pass you

por - tant like a moun - tain or tall like a tree.

When green is all there is to be, it could make you

won - der why. But why won - der, why won - der? I am green, and it'-ll do fine._ It's

beau - ti - ful,_ and I think it's what I want to be. _____

NEARLY MISSED

Words and music by Joe Raposo

Light rock

D7　Bm/A　D9　Bm/A　D7　Bm/A　D9　Bm/D

with Pedal

D7　Bm/A　D9　D6　Am

While look - in' at my feet at a crack in the side - walk, an

old tin can by the side of the road, __ I near - ly missed a

1. rain - bow, __ I near - ly missed a sun - set, I near - ly missed a
2. rain - bow. __ Don't wan-na miss a rain - bow! __ I would-n't miss a

shoo-ting star go - in' by. __ While stud - y - in' a brand-new

hole in my snea-ker, and fin - din' a quar-ter and an old bus to - ken,

I near-ly missed a rain-bow,___ I near-ly missed a sun-set,___

I near-ly missed a shoo-ting star___ go-in' by.___

Look-in' down at the ground___ means you know where you're go - in',___

___ no head up in the clouds___ to lead you a - stray,

PICTURE A WORLD

Words and music by Joe Raposo

Pic-ture a world __ of hon-ey-warm haze

and the wind play-ing tag __ in the play-ground trees __

__ on sum-mer days, __ and try to think of a way __

__ to make it that way.

Brown frog tal - kin' to a ___ but - ter - fly; ___ flow-ers grow-in'
oh, so high; ___ skies wide o - pen, stars so near, ___ just
reach up and touch one from here. ___ Ev' - ry-bod - y
pic - ture a world ___ where lit - tle kids run, ___

93

where the sun-shine is pour – ing love__ and life__ on ev' – ry – one,

and try to think of a way_____ to make it

that way,_____ make it that way,_____

__ make it that way._____

I LOVE TRASH

Words and music by Jeffrey Moss

rot - ten or rus - ty;_____ oh, I love trash!_____

1. I have here a snea-ker that's tat-tered and worn; it's all full of
2. I have here some news-pa-per, thir-teen months old. I've wrapped fish in-
3. I've a clock that won't work and an old tel-e-phone, a bro-ken um-

holes, and the la-ces are torn — a gift from my moth-er the day I was
side it; it's smel-ly and cold; but I would-n't trade it for a big pot of
brel-la, a rus-ty trom-bone, and I am de-ligh-ted to call them my

born. I love it be - cause it's trash. Yes,
gold. I love it be - cause it's trash. Yes,
own. I love them be - cause they're trash. Oh,

I love, I _____

_____ love trash! _____

WALK DOWN THE STREET
(WITH YOUR HEAD UP HIGH)

Words and music by Jeffrey Moss

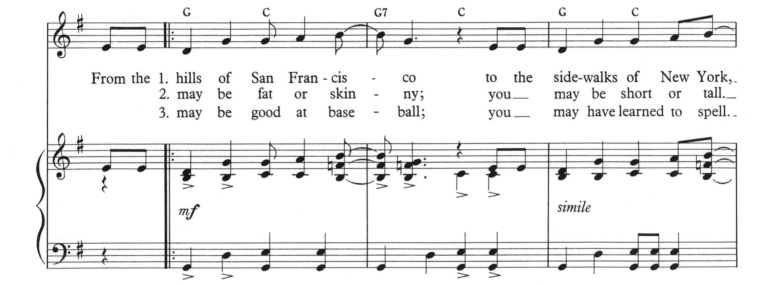

From the 1. hills of San Fran - cis - co to the side-walks of New York,
2. may be fat or skin - ny; you__ may be short or tall.__
3. may be good at base - ball; you__ may have learned to spell.__

when - ev - er you're walk - ing__ down the street, well, there's
What - ev - er you are,__ well, I like you fine,_ and you
Who - ev - er you are,__ well, you've got your thing, so__

98

just one_ way to walk:_ You've got to
don't have to change at all. _ So go and walk down the street with your
just try to do it real well._ Then you can

head up high._ Keep a cool look of con-fi-dence in your eye._ You know that

noth-ing's im-pos-si-ble if you try,_ so go and walk down the street with your

head up high!

You
You

You're an ex-tra-spe-cial per-son, and if you want to trav-el far,__

__ well, be good, be kind, but keep in mind__ to be

proud of what-ev-er you are. Yeah, go and walk down the street with your

100

head up high._ Keep a cool look of con-fi-dence in your eye._ You know that

noth-ing is im-pos-si-ble if you try,_ so go and walk down the street with your

head up high! Keep your head up

high! Keep your head_ up_ high!_

Cadenza

ad lib.

RAIN FALLS

Words by Jeffrey Moss · Music by Joe Raposo

Rain falls___ soft-ly on the ground, help-ing all the flow-ers grow.
Rain falls___ pud-dles on the street, No one can go out and play.

Rain falls,_ pret-ty rain-drops all a-round, help-ing riv-ers start to flow.
Rain falls_ peo-ple soaked from head to feet, Gee, I like a rain-y day.

Streets get clean be-fore the rain_ is done, and
Trucks roll by, splash mud on ev'-ry-one. You

SING

Words and music by Joe Raposo

loud;   sing out strong.

Sing   of good things, not bad;   sing of

hap-py, not sad.   Sing!   Sing a

song.   Make it sim-ple, to last your whole life

long. _____ Don't wor-ry that it's not good e-nough for

an - y - one else to hear. Sing! Sing a

song. _____ La - la - do - la - da - la, da - la - do - la - da - la,

da - da - la - do - la - da. _____ La - do - la - da - la, da - la - la - da - lo,

SOMEDAY LITTLE CHILDREN

Words and music by Jeffrey Moss

moon. Yeah, peo - ple liv - in' on the moon_ some - day.
strong. Yeah, peo - ple ain't gon - na get sick_ no_ more.
love. Yeah, a world of peace and love_ some - day.

Are you won - der - in'___ who?
It sounds a - maz - ing, but it's true.
To last a hun - dred life - times through.

Well, I'll tell you, lit - tle chil - dren: It just might_ be
You know who's gon - na see it hap - pen? Well, it might_ be
You know who's gon - na make it hap - pen? Well, it's gon - na be

come ___ some - day,   Come on,

some - day!   come on,___ some - day!___

SPEƆIAL

Words and music by Jeffrey Moss

Easily

No - bo - dy's eyes are quite the same as your eyes. Some eyes are brown, and

some are big and blue. But your eyes are spec - ial just be-cause they're your eyes,

and you are spec - ial just be-cause you're you.

No - bo -dy's voice sounds quite the same as your voice, sing - ing or laugh - ing or

call - ing out my name. Your voice is spec - ial just be-cause it's your voice.

No oth - er voice sounds quite the same. You're

113

some - bo - dy spec - ial; there's no - bo - dy like you. You won't find an-oth - er if you

trav - el far and wide. You've got your own spec - ial feel -ings, Your own spec - ial se -crets, Your

own spec - ial hap - pi-ness deep__ in - side. — And

no - bo-dy's smile shines quite the same as your smile; no - bo-dy can smile

just the way you do. Your smile is spe - cial just be-cause it's your smile,

and you are spec - ial just be-cause you're you._____ You're the

one and___ on - ly ex - t'ror - di - na - ry ve - ry spe - cial

you._____

THE GARDEN

Words and music by Joe Raposo

mix it up good with a pop-si-cle stick and an old pa-per cup you found.
mix it up good with a die-sel truck and bl-ow it ev'ry-where.

Add an emp-ty tube of tooth-paste and dump it
Now add a dash of ha-zy sun-shine pee-kin' through a

mess things up,___ that you can clean up the mess___ be - fore it

mess - es up me! You take a lot of trash and dump it in the

bot - tom of the sea.___ The oc - to - pus - es and the

oy - sters won't com - plain to you and me.___ But___ some day you might get

hun-gry _____ for a tu-na fric-as-see _____ and you've got a

G7   C7   A7   D7

1. glop,   glop,   grun-gy glop   gar-den ___   where the   o-cean   used to ___ be. ___
2. glop,   glop,   grun-gy glop   gar-den ___   where the   flow-ers   used to ___ be. ___
3. glop,   glop,   grun-gy glop   gar-den ___   where the   play-ground used to ___ be. ___
4. glop,   glop,   grun-gy glop   gar-den ___   where the   whole world used to ___ be! ___

1,2,3
G   C7   4   G   C   G7

I say you've got a ___   Oh,   yes!

RUBBER DUCKIE

Words and music by Jeffrey Moss

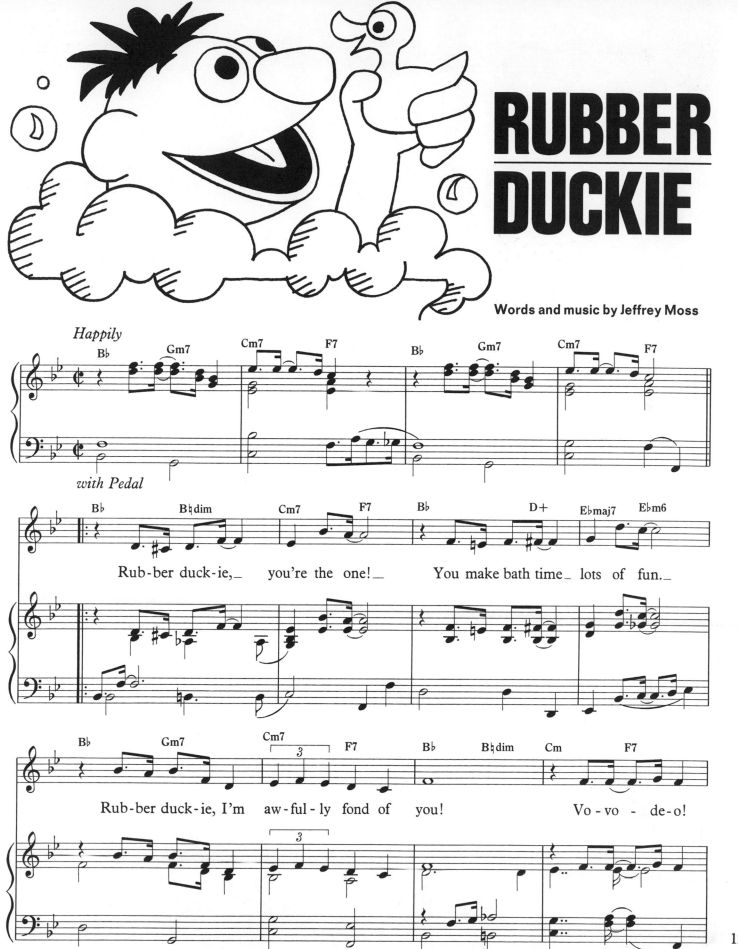

Rub-ber duck-ie,_ you're the one!_ You make bath time_ lots of fun._

Rub-ber duck-ie, I'm aw-ful-ly fond of you! Vo-vo-de-o!

Rub - ber duck-ie,— joy of joys,— when I squeeze you,— you make noise.—

Rub - ber duck-ie, you're my ver - y best friend, it's true. Oh,

ev' - ry day, when I make my way to the tub - by,— I find a

lit - tle fel - low who's cute and yel - low and chub - by.—

Rub - a - dub - dub - by!__ Rub - ber duck - ie,__ you're so fine,__

and I'm luck-y__ that you're mine! Rub-ber duck-ie, I'm aw-ful-ly fond_of

you! rub-ber duck-ie, I'd like a whole pond_of,

rub-ber duck-ie, I'm aw-ful-ly fond_ of you!_____

123

SOMEBODY COME AND PLAY

Words and music by Joe Raposo

Some-bod-y come and play.___ Some-bod-y come and play to-day.___

Some-bod-y come and smile the smiles and sing the songs. It won't take long.

Some-bod-y come and play___ to-day._____

124

Some-bod-y come and play. __ Some-bod-y come and play my way. __

Some-bod-y come and rhyme the rhymes and laugh the laughs. It won't take long.

Some-bod-y come and play __ to-day. _____

Some-bod-y come with me and see the plea-sure in the wind.

Some-bod-y come be - fore it gets too late to be - gin. ___

Some-bod-y come and play. ___ Some-bod-y come and play to-day. ___

Some-bod-y come and be my friend and watch the sun till it rains ___ a - gain.

Some-bod-y come and play to-day. ___

INDEX OF SONGS

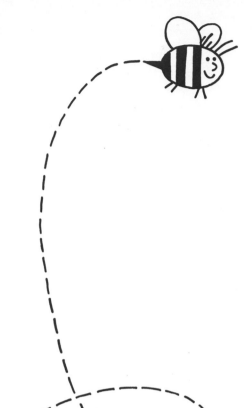

INDEX OF FIRST LINES